ALL ONE BREATH

ALL ONE BREATH

poems

ROBERT PACK

GREEN WRITERS PRESS *Brattleboro, Vermont*

Printed in the United States

10 9 8 7 6 5 4 3 2 1

Green Writers Press is a Vermont-based publisher whose mission is to spread a message of hope and renewal through the words and images we publish. Throughout, we will adhere to our commitment to preserving and protecting the natural resources of the earth. To that end, a percentage of our proceeds will be donated to environmental activist groups. Green Writers Press gratefully acknowledges support from individual donors, friends, and readers to help support the environment and our publishing initiative.

Giving Voice to Writers Who Will Make the World a Better Place
Green Writers Press | Brattleboro, Vermont
www.greenwriterspress.com

ISBN: 978-0-9987012-9-5

COVER PHOTO: ERIK PACK

PRINTED ON PAPER WITH PULP THAT COMES FROM FSC-CERTIFIED FORESTS, MANAGED FORESTS THAT GUARANTEE RESPONSIBLE ENVIRONMENTAL, SOCIAL, AND ECONOMIC PRACTICES BY LIGHTNING. SOURCE ALL WOOD PRODUCT COMPONENTS USED IN BLACK & WHITE, STANDARD COLOR, OR SELECT COLOR PAPERBACK BOOKS, UTILIZING EITHER CREAM OR WHITE BOOKBLOCK PAPER, THAT ARE MANUFACTURED IN THE LAVERGNE, TENNESSEE PRODUCTION CENTER ARE SUSTAINABLE FORESTRY INITIATIVE® (SFI®) CERTIFIED SOURCING.

For that which befalleth the sons of men befalleth the beasts; as the one dieth, so dieth the other; yea, they all have one breath.

ECCLESIASTES, THREE

For Talli Ebin and John Glendenning

CONTENTS

❧

FOREWORD

❦

WHAT AN EXTRAORDINARY GIFT Robert Pack, who has blessed us with poems for the past sixty-three years, has given us in this, his most recent volume! Where to begin?

There's the eco-friendly Bob Pack, heir to the tradition of Wordsworth. You can feel the very air of Montana in these poems: in the snow geese returning home once again, in the dwindled herds of Montana bison, in the poignant image of his daughter, Pamela, existentially alone on one of those mountain cliffs she has been climbing over the years, hanging on only by her fingers and toes hundreds of feet above ground level as a hawk sails hovering below her and evening comes on.

Then too there are the poems with his son, Erik, helping his aging father settle into a canoe, the two rowing out into the glacial lake, or hiking high in the pine- and birch-studded mountains. And other poems as well, in which the poet's grandson figures, the old man eager to teach the boy how to pitch a curveball or field a grounder. There are those heart-wrenching memories of the father the poet lost at a too-young age and of an aging mother and of a beloved sister back there in the Bronx all those years ago, and soon we, too, are caught up in the web of life's unenviable and inevitable losses.

Add to these Pack's poignantly comic poems, as when an old man admires the nearly-transcendent beauty of a young woman, or the old man making his way to his front door at Halloween to find a masked woman in an erotic hallucination whispering "trick or treat," as the old man tries to figure what to do with that.

Then the poems to and about Patty, his wife for as long as he's been writing his poems. The truth is his humor and wit and kindness have been mainstays for me now for nearly half a century. Along with his George Burns/ Jack Benny humor and his outrageous puns, the way he packs his poems with puns over and over. As in *Sing, heavenly moose*, which, when he read it in Bread Loaf's Little Theatre years ago the poet Marvin Bell got up and booed him (with affection of course) until everyone, as it dawned on them what Pack—straight-faced of course—had just done, rose up and joined the chorus.

To counter this comedic strain, there's the philosophical Pack, constantly questioning the meaning of it all, questioning God (if in your world—as in Berryman's or Hardy's or Frost's poetry—there is a God for you to address) even as the years and months and days slip from us, urging us to make up our minds while there's still time. For me, at least, Pack's poems keep echoing a recurrent theme from the Book of Ecclesiastes, which is something he and I across the table have mused upon and discussed so many times over the years, most recently in Rabbi Ravi Shapiro's translation, "For that which befalleth the sons of men befalleth the beasts..."

And then there are those allusions to Freud and Darwin, whom he has studied over the years, as well as his long interior dialogues with his old pals, Shakespeare and Milton and Keats.

And of course there's the language: the sheer sublimity of his evocations of nature, as Harold Bloom noted years ago, a language filled with the beauty and sadness inherent in our consonants and vowels. It's a language which for me evokes the worlds of Hart Crane's *White Buildings* and Wallace Stevens's *Auroras of Autumn*. Or think of Charlie Chaplin or Jimmy Durante, saying goodbye to his audience, then turning and fading away as he exits, while the circle of the screen narrows and then—inevitably—goes black.

There are so many wonderful stories he has given us over the years, which go hand in hand, as they must, with the very way in which he tells those stories, whether in trimeters or tetrameters or pentameters, Formalist that he is. His sonnets strike me as so subtle and so right, like his rhymed stanzas and his mastery of the blank verse line. And, as always, there's the straightforward way he enters into a poem, something which reminds me time and time again of one of his favorites, Robert Frost:

> Driving me home from yet
> another visit to the eye doctor,

my wife took the old farmland route,
and there across a field of corn,
stretching from east to west,
a rainbow's arc appeared . . .

And we're back to the world of Noah and Genesis and Leviticus once more, and that heard and unheard music suffused with the poet's profound understanding of suffering. Not only human suffering, but the suffering of animals, who have no language with which to express their suffering, beyond a howl or whimper or—more poignantly—silence.

And then there's his wife Patty again, helping him back into the house and standing him on his walker, old soldier that he is, with a storm outside threatening to drown everything. And then, voila!, the beautiful dreamlike ending of the book, where Patty opens the door to let the animals in, two by two: "the white-tailed deer,/ foxes and wolves, red squirrels, bobcats," and the frolicking rest.

Here then is our covenant with creation: to care for the vulnerable. All of which somehow manages to touch on the beauty and majesty of what Bob Pack's poems have wrought for us yet one more time. These poems, dear reader, are a powerful testament to the human imagination, poems where I can hear Stevens and Yeats and even canny Shakespeare applauding, there, somewhere in the rafters, in those rumbling sounds that seem to speak like thunder.

Paul Mariani
January 2018

ALL ONE BREATH

SNOW GEESE RETURNING

Standing on the shore of Freezeout Lake
This March here in Montana I observe
Snow geese migrating back to Canada
Where they will court and mate and feed

Upon succulent weeds. And I can see
A coasting row of geese upon the lake
Maybe a mile long, thirty across—
Ten thousand curving forms repeating there.

Each gliding in its self-appointed place
Just barely touching side by feathered side,
Aglow, aglitter, incandescent in
The glorifying, unobstructed sun.

Who is this shimmering designed to please,
This fine effulgence of reflected light?
What kind of fabricator would contrive
This scene to help a witness like myself

Put darker, melancholy thoughts aside,
Thoughts of companions never to return,
Never to see migrating geese again—
The thrust of their stretched bodies blurred by flight

A sudden surge of black-tipped wings ascends
To startled tumult in the air, and I—
Lift up celebrating hands to join
This flourishing of animated sky.

WELCOMING FAREWELL

A cornucopia for winter birds,
our feeder welcomes nuthatches and chickadees
as snow ghosts hunker down in hemlock trees.
From silence they emerge which frames the words
we whisper in our fluted welcoming
to the arriving nuthatches and chickadees—
as if their coming is designed to please
our wish to share their company. And yet they bring
to mind the murmur of midsummer bees
that sparkled in a purple clover field.
The seasons merge as rumbling bees now yield
to snow ghosts silent in the hemlock trees
and we—attuned to disappearing wings,
the fluttering of nuthatches and chickadees,
the choiring harmony of honey bees,
their muted undertones, their murmurings—
we summon phrases of farewell to call
to the departing nuthatches and chickadees,
farewell to drowsy dragonflies and bees,
farewell to umber flare-up in effulgent fall,
in welcoming fresh silence that embraces bees,
embraces the translucent dragonfly, the whir
and thrum of the exhausted grasshopper,
and all quick nuthatches and chickadee.
bodes well for everyone.

NATIONAL BISON RANGE, MONTANA

for Pat Burke

Before the nineteenth century began
with the absurd assumption
Nature's resources are unlimited,
some sixty million bison grazed
the grasslands of our continent,
Western prairies stretched out
in the horizon's haze
where orange sunsets bleed
on snow-covered mountaintops.

Hunted by settlers and by Indians,
whole herds were soon exterminated;
in a hundred fleeting years
their desiccated skulls were stacked
in towers to witness their shared fate.
The wolves who preyed on bison calves,
the injured, or the frail,
suffered a loss of sustenance
as human populations grew
and prospered, and it only took
another hundred years before the bison,
terrified and fleeing, were then driven
over gaping precipices almost to
extinction's blank finality.

Their best survival strategy—
ironically in retrospect—

would have been to appeal
to homo sapiens, like wolves
who learned to guard our fires
in exchange for scraps of meat;
ten-thousand years ago they
morphed into domestic dogs.

Too big, not cute enough, and high
in protein, bison seemed destined to be
eliminated from the earth until
a savior, Teddy Roosevelt,
conceived the idea of a park
where bison could survive and multiply.

Call it a mystery—the reverence for life,
call it fortuitous, but something new
in the unfolding saga of
sustaining habitats—protecting,
peaceful, and secure—appeared
beneath the blaze of the indifferent sun—
a fabrication, mindfully designed—
deliberate and purposeful, and yet composed
only of water, earth, and air,
of seasons cycling and of leaves flashing
their effulgent colors in the wind.

So from this swooning height,
I look out at the flowing vistas
leading down steep rolling slopes
of incandescent yarrow fields,

each cluster of the tiny flowers
like miniature galaxies.
The swirl of space across a valley
winds to a river of smooth silver light
reflected from the current of the air
and radiates an inner silver of its own
before receding into azure shade.
There on the vaulted mountainside,
now shimmering with gold balsamroot
oblivious, composed, and still,
a dozen mighty bison graze;
among them bounds a tawny calf
as if it were the first calf ever born.

     A meadowlark is singing on the fence
that frames the border of the park,
expressing my heart's conviction
that this day with my own son,
with Pat and Dan, my cherished friends—
caretakers of the wilderness—
will end well.

LEVIATHAN ARISING

Almost four billion years have emptied out
since life emerged to fill the seas
and populate the trimming earth,
and yet no creature has survived
beyond its flashing moment in the sun,
though I can picture them in passing,
all parading with their ornaments.

Creating forms that look as if
they are designed to last
is improvising Nature's specialty—
like the Blue whale now plundered
almost to extinction's edge,
the largest creature ever to display
astounding gracefulness, at peace
with what its body's bulk permits.

And we, despite our yearning
for unchanging permanence,
as if our kind could be released
from the excruciations of all flesh—
so that our longing to survive
enabled us to see ourselves reborn,
emerging once again to grope our way
through drowsy mists of primal dawn.

And yet I know that I must banish hope
for still another life to come so I'll
be free to celebrate impermanence
and free to grieve without the fantasy
of happiness sustained in paradise.

How can rampaging wind,
as if it were a dragon's breath
that topples trees and blasts
receding rows of corn be other than
indifferent to our needs and our desires?

Transience alone that leads the mind
past loss into forgetfulness,
is able to assuage the vanishing
of parents and of friends, years merging
into undistinguishable years.
whose memories we may possess,
but only in the vanishing.

When was it that I wandered restless
on that weed-entangled shore
and watched leviathan heave up its bulk,
its luminescent fins and back,
above its buoyant element
before it plunged and disappeared,
framed by blown, swirling spume,
the smack of its spread tail
resounding through the universe?

GRIN AND BEAR IT

He rose at dawn as usual,
stretched his thick limbs,
and did what bears always have done
and thought what bears always have thought.
    He peed to reassert this was his property,
gorged on a ripened huckleberry bush,
scratched on a tree to sharpen his hooked claws,
then bounded off until he reached
the forest's scrubby borderline,
    Beside a road he came upon
an empty car from which a scent
must have attracted him.
With one swipe of its handle he
opened the door and rumbled in,
then sat himself on the front seat.
Somehow the door swung closed;
somehow he must have leaned
against the upright lock
thus shutting himself in.
He sat there with his paws upon
the steering wheel, gazing
ahead into the dappled light.
    If only he knew what to do
to get the engine started, knew
what he should pull and what to push,
he would be able to head out
to some new destiny,
to venture where no bear had ever gone.

But that, alas, was not to be.
He'd reached an evolutionary
halting in place, a terminal plateau.
        And that is where I make my entry
in this elemental scene.
Just driving by, I spied the bear
in his predicament
and knew he knew I knew
I was responsible to rescue him.
Help is what people do—
at least when we are so inclined
as I was happily inclined that day.
        I pried the door latch loose
with a big crow-bar that I carried
for emergencies
and the humungous bear.
sensing benign intent,
paused for a moment and then hurtled out.
I felt his rough fur brush against my arm
as he escaped returning to bear
territory in the woods.
        Self-satisfied, I revved the
engine of my car
and sped back home
to do what people always do,
to think what people always think,
to tell a disillusioned friend
my story of the rescued bear.

DACTYLLIC PUNISHMENT

Monkey glands, monkey glands,
William Yeats, troubadour,
Can old age still offer
Sex that is fun?
Summon your potency
Cardiovascular,
Shoot for an heir who's a
Son of a Gonne.

❧

Money-lust, money-lust,
Thomas Stearns Eliot,
Drove you to London where
Culture abounds.
Squeezing the Waste Land out,
Analerotically,
Your turgid references,
Did make you pounds.

❧

Pastoral, pastoral.
Wordsworth, thou wanderer,
How do the fields bring you
Innocent bliss?
Or are the daffodils,
Photosynthetically,
Doing a dance that re-
Minds you of Sis?

Courtesy, courtesy,
Poets bi-sexual,
How do you manage to
Find time to write?
Beat down those energies
Hyperandrogynous,
Set yourself limits of,
One page a knight.

Oedipus, shmedipus,
Sigmund Freud, analyst,
Polymorph-perverse and
Sexually hip,
Is your mom posing there
Photogenetically,
Silkily dressed in a
Freudian slip?

Polyglot, polyglot,
Bernard Shaw, dramatist,
Teaching phonetics must
Sure turn you on.
Urgently amorous
Hyperloquacity
Made you a chauvinist
Pygmalion.

DARWIN'S TESTAMENT

When Darwin reached old age after
a lifelong malady that drained his strength
and caused him nausea that interfered
with innovative researches on worms
or barnacles or climbing plants,
he'd ask his wife at evening by the fire
to read to him out loud from a worn book
he was assured concluded happily.
Surely there was sufficient suffering
in daily life even for those who felt
adversity can strengthen character,
thus giving purpose to what might appear
inscrutably evil, though such belief,
congenial to human pride, did not,
he knew, apply to animals who lack
consoling words to ease starvation or
the grip of a determined predator.
Though evolution brought forth varied forms
most beautiful to contemplate—a process
   Darwin described as having "grandeur,"
his awed sense of Nature's plenitude
was superseded by the evidence
of Nature's cruelty and waste
and then confirmed beyond remaining doubt
when his beloved Annie died of fever
that parental care could not abate
at only ten years old, without
an outcry of protest by her to shake
the smooth striation buried in the hills.

And yet it brought him joy to understand
how natural selection could create
uncanny patterns and resemblances,
expressions of contentment or of fear
on human faces everywhere
across the separating continents
in children, and in chimpanzees.
 The shaded colorings of finches' wings,
the varied sizes of their beaks,
enabled Darwin to forget his gloom;
he took delight in adaptations like
a frog that's capable of climbing trees,
a fish that can change sexes if
a sudden mating opportunity
presents itself, a forest bird
that feigns it has a broken wing
in order to distract a stalking fox
from sniffing out its nest of naked chicks.
 How plants respond to stimuli
engaged his boundless curiosity,
so Darwin had his son Francis improvise
on his bassoon beside the close plant
domesticated in his care. I like
to think he heard it whispering its thanks.
All living things, he was convinced at heart,
composed one single seamless family
and shared a single origin.
 Darwin had solved the deepest mystery
of how new species could evolve without
the intervention of divinity,
and thus the mystery of humankind,

yet the enigma of his own unique
identity as witness to our being here,
his joy, endurance, and his suffering,
remains elusive to our enquiry.
Perhaps his malady was caused
by some germ he contracted on
his youthful, five-year journey
in tropical South America
or in the unexplored Galapagos.
Or maybe he had violated some
inherent innocence of Nature with
forbidden knowledge symbolized
as in the fatal apple scrutinized
in outcast Adam's reaching hand
whose consequences only could be
understood too late to remedy.

    Is this the burden of his testament—
knowledge of how we've been created to
become the conscious creatures we now are,
desiring permanence, enthralled by change,—
green shadings of transfigured green—
successfully surviving for a while?

GIVING THANKS

Two ponderosa pines define
the entryway that leads—
this clear and midday afternoon—
down to the shore of Holland Lake.
My son helps lift my outworn body
over the smooth gunnel of our fishing boat,
and off we go in the direction of
the gliding loons who dip and disappear,
leaving behind the lilting echoes
of their melancholy calls.
Framed by a cloud, an eagle
streaks toward its enormous nest
above the forest maze
and misty labyrinth.
      The mountain on the lake's far side
offers meadow of gold Balsamroot;
a pregnant doe lifts up her head,
pausing at the water's boundary.
About four boat lengths past
the swirl where the resounding waterfall
foams out and merges with the lake,
a cove reveals a beaver's hutch
remarkably symmetrical—
each branch and twig packed into place—
suggesting some unchangeable design
has been revealed to me.
Simply to look, to hold in memory,
was all that my senses needed to achieve,
and all wished-for contentment could embrace.

But not quite so—such satisfaction
left still more to be desired:
    I needed to express
imagined gratitude
for pulsing light reflected from
round purple stones that murmured
with the undulating tide.
I needed to bestow high praise,
as if such praise could be received
and sheltered safely in the forest haze;
I needed to give thanks for symmetry,
and all its variants
in the unfolding Aspen leaves,
in the emerging needles
nearly shining row by row
on the awakened Tamaracks.
I needed to commend
the shaded slopes and crevices
for their fine tints and multimarked hues;
I was uplifted and impelled
to offer unrequited praise
for the melodic interlude
of disappearing loons—
as if such mournful singing was
an unanticipated gift beyond.

THE FINE ART

If an aged genie, liberated from
A purple bottle washed up on a beach,
Granted the wish to live my life again,
I'd save events mainly as they occurred,
So I've decided to make only
Minor revisions in my life to come.
    I'll add a few percentage points to my
School batting averages so that the strict
Demands of pride are met, though I suspect
I still will need to fantasize brand new
Startling statistics to console me for
The championship game we lost by just
A single run, observed in the loud stands
By a girl, hooded in cascading hair,
Who disappeared into the swirling crowd.
    So maybe I'll need more revisions than
I'd previously thought. I'll have
To add some doubles in the record book,
Some triples, homers, a walk-off grand slam
For my admiring fans to memorize.
My epitaph engraved in stone will read:
Here rests Bob Pack, now lift your eyes,
For he alone on a good day
could go a barren 0 for 4
and see his batting average rise.
    Defying the restrictive laws of math,
I will achieve a consummation in
Comic accordance with what's possible
In the extravagance of wishfulness.

I'll coach my only grandson the fine art
Of how to hit, so he'll achieve a new
Identity to guide him on his way.
I'll hope that in the open, long home stretch
Walking alone along a gleaming beach
Of colored glass and fractured spiral shells,
Where spume swirl murmurs what the genie meant,
My grandson, in remaining years, will need
Only the lightest insubstantial touch
Of improvised embellishment.

SWIMMER

I can't recall where I was coming from,
or where my destination led,
or what was motivating me,
something elusively interior,
too deep for consciousness to grasp?
I passed a row of cherry trees
and found myself on a back road
that wound to a deserted space to park
and then to a dirt pathway down
to meet a solitary beach beside
a sparkling lake at least two miles across
with no one that I could discern
on the far shore. I don't know why
I felt such urgency, but I stripped down
to just my underwear and plunged right in
as if a voice commanded me.
I had long muscles for a steady kick,
sinewy shoulders for my stroke,
and I believed no distance was beyond
what I could will myself to swim across
simply because the lake was there,
because the water welcomed me.
It was midsummer, and the evening sun
was on my left, due west, so when
I lifted my outstretching arm
and turned my head to seize a breath,
the setting orange sun ignited
the translucent water globes
cascading from my hand and down my arm

and made it seem as if
a multitude of miniature suns,
each one in its own universe,
all setting yet suspended in
their vanishing, surrounded and
illuminated my appearance there
in the brief moment of its happening.
I can't recall arriving on
the other shore, although I may have seen
a lantern waving there to signal me.
nor am I able to remember how
I managed to return to find my car.
All that survives that I can bring to mind
is how my self-propelling body felt—
buoyant, untiring, and at one
with its smooth, rhythmic gliding through
the lake's embracing element.
I still can see the incandescent sun
reflected in each dripping globe
that tumbled from the high arc of my arm
with every measured stroke I took
to nowhere in my mind except
my body's being wholly where it was.
I can't describe the shaded room
in which, distracted, I awoke to find
a newspaper with an account
of an unlikely drowning in
the very lake that I had visited—
was it only the day before?

The dead man was not recognized
by the local authorities
who had no evidence that might reveal
why he had come alone to this
cliff-hidden valley and this lake.
Was he not used to swimming distances;
had he misjudged his stamina
or his incentive to reveal himself?
And I—I wonder if I can explain
to anyone who still remains perplexed
or to my own astonished questioning.
what drew me to that isolated lake
the youthful summer that I found myself
afloat in self-forgetfulness,
although I certainly remember
the descending orange sun ablaze
in its vibrating radiance.
What can it be, can it have been
that rose up out of emptiness
from some unfathomable depth
behind my eyes, but my sense of
miraculously being there
by choice, by chance, by serendipity,
illuminated by the setting sun,
repeated and contained in each
ripe water drop, my temporarily
immortal body, perfectly alive,
my last, best claim of worthiness?

TRUE ENOUGH

I had not read my poems in public
any time before, and afterwards
a lady came up to the podium
and said, "how terrible." I thought she meant
the poems themselves, but when she took my hand
I realized she meant my poem
about a hunting accident
in which I stumble on a fallen branch
and shoot my brother in the back.
His death was what evoked her sympathy.
"But I don't have a brother," I declared,
"I made the story up for the poem's sake,
its need to entertain, and I depicted him as my own twin
with all the rivalry that would imply.
I modeled him on someone I once knew."
You mean you lied!" she snorted in my face.
and roughly yanked away her hand.

II
A day arrived when, wishing to expand
my narrow image of myself,
I started writing monologues
from other people's points of view—
invented characters with lives
that differed widely from my own,
some desperate and some serene,
including women in the privacy
of their desires and their regrets.

I read a poem whose speaker was
a woman lying in her bed at night
as slatted moonlight streamed in through the blinds,
nursing her infant boy, enjoying
the warm fullness of her breasts while picturing
the faces of the men that she had loved
as if in turn they all were nursing there.
    After the reading, an offended student
angrily accosted me: "How dare you, a man,
assume that you can understand
what women feel?" I stuttered a response,
and then, no doubt assisted by
my female muse, I leaned toward her
and whispered in her ear that previous
to my sex re-assignment surgery,
I had inhabited a body that
I was not suited for, although
        I well remember how that body felt,
its longings and anxieties.
I had suspected she suspected I
was counting on some basic human
instinct for credulity and guessed
she didn't want to take the chance
she might be wrong in doubting me.
So with a flourish she apologized.
and I assured her I took no offense,
and hoped she'd buy a copy of my book.

III
        A friend by chance stumbled upon
a recently published poem of mine,

written in the first person singular.
about a married couple's long-delayed
vacation in a fishing village up
in northern Maine, known for its lobster hauls.
its crabs, its moody bayside vistas
as grey, intermittent morning gusts
inflated snapping sails with orange light
and filled the air with squawking gulls
as if the scene had wished to be described.
     The day that they drive home could not have been
more beautiful or more serene
and yet, implausibly, they get
into an argument about how much
the State should give aid to the destitute.
The question whether excess empathy—
whatever excess might imply—
can weaken independence in
the innocent recipient, released
in them some hidden animosity.
To their astonishment, more anger
than they would have thought was possible
bitterly came streaming forth.
"Sorry you had a blowout with your wife,"
the friend wrote in compassionate response,
"but arguments occur in marriages.
     Therapy helped when my relationship
with Ruth began to fail. Below you'll find
the name and number of our analyst
who tells me he too is divorced, though maybe
that's his strategy to win my trust."
I wrote right back informing him

I had contrived the crazy argument
because it gave my poem dramatic heft
and psychic interest, although
I really do not know how best
to help the poor or if they are to blame—
or you, or I, or anyone.
In any case, I hope you liked my poem,
especially the vivid image of
the orange sails puffed out at dawn,
And thanks for your blunt brotherly advice."

IV

And now, dear reader, I assume
that you would like to know if these
historical accounts indeed are true,
or if I fabricated them as an excuse
to flaunt my flair for meter pulsing
its iambic beats dee dum dee dum
just like a living human heart.
But here's another explanation,
much too serious to be expressed
without some mitigating mirth,
for my improvisations on the facts
of my depictions of my life as if
to conjure myself up in jester's garb
with curling shoes, a dropping cap,
and button bells along red sleeves.
And yes, this portrait must suffice to ease
your apprehensions and to soothe your dreams.
With only mischievous elaborations of
a script not of my making or design,

just chance, just accident, just randomness.
it offers you an alternate to fate.

     Between two incarnations when I had
the opportunity to ask the Lord
why there is so much suffering on earth,
why bad things happen to the virtuous,
the Lord replied that "suffering
is the authentic soul, with mortal time
so very brief, of your humanity;
sorrow makes your best stories grip the mind
of the rapt listener, inspiring
holy empathy. This is the comfort
that I offer you: one equalizing
destiny that everyone can share,
embrace, yet, in embracing, made your own."

     I started to protest—"such consolation
leaves the overflow of sorrow unredeemed"—and,
desperate,
I improvised a joke reminding Him
that it was I who had invented Him
in the composure of His majesty.
But He was on a roll and would not be
cajoled or interrupted... So
to give Him a concluding rhyme—
since everything must have an end—
a rhyme I patiently have saved till now,
I'll have Him contemplate His beard and say:
"What happens here in heaven is complete
in being what it is without revision
or embellishment. It's no surprise
there is no poetry in Paradise."

BASEBALL IN ELYSIUM

Seventy years ago today,
the captain of our high school baseball team,
I came to bat in our concluding game
with two runs down, three men on base,
two outs, the bottom of the ninth.

The pitcher threw his heater down the pike
as counter power surged up from my thighs
into my back, my shoulders, and my arms,
exploding in a smoothly perfect swing—
a thud loud as a thunderclap
that drove the ball beyond the left field fence
and out of sight. I think it might
be streaking still like a slick meteor.

Dorothy was watching from the stands,
whose name in Greek means "gift of God"
which I learned when I memorized
Wordsworth's long poem about his sister
wading in a stream of purple stones
whatever that might signify about
the flow of murmuring impermanence.

I still can see her lift her frilly skirt
above the leaping foam, showing her knees
like apples in the leafy, speckled light
She must have been impressed by my
Homeric feat that afternoon that seemed
to have a sheen beyond forgetfulness.

Yes, baseball and its rooting fans
must thrive in paradise, season after
scorekeeping season still unwinding
toward a consummating end
with everyone's statistics finally
determining their resting place.

I think I'll come to bat again against
the fastball pitcher I had faced
that championship high school game
in which I homered with the bases full,
two strikes on me, and three on base
the bottom of the roaring ninth.

I hope I hadn't cast a shadow
on his boyhood memory, his sense
of what distinguished him, with dark defeat
locked in his heart. Perhaps I should
apologize to him as if somehow
the two of us were interchangeable,
each other's complement, although

I'm sure the record books are fixed
and can't be qualified, can't be revised
despite how legends will embellish what
already may be fabulous.
But this analysis is dubious
with failure graven in the mind;
defeat and triumph are not absolutes.

Maybe he'd claim his recollection of
his getting clobbered in the ninth
is his wife's favorite because he learned
a needed lesson in humility,
that even his best pitch was hittable.
And maybe Dorothy is her true name,
not merely a coincidence, as if
a gift of some bemused intelligence.
And there he hovers on the mound,

Elysium's gold light enfolding him,
twirling the baseball in his pitching hand
concealed from scrutiny behind his back,
arranging the rough ridges of the seams,
his left foot planted on the rubber as
he glares at me. What will he throw this time:
his slider or his change-up, or—
a jocular retelling of the past
inspired by a transcendent itch for fame—
a brush-back pitch quite close enough
to let me know we've not yet reached eternity?

TALMUDIC EXEGISIS

*And the Lord said to Moses, Thou canst not see my face: for
there shall no man see me, and live. And the Lord said, Behold,
there is a place by me, and thou shalt stand upon a rock: And it
shall come to pass, while my glory passeth by, that I will put thee
in a cleft of the rock, and will cover thee with my hand while I
pass by: And I will take away mine hand, and thou shalt see my
back parts: but my face shall not be seen.*

EXODUS 33

So too with us, the human face
is dangerous to look upon,
Of all the body's parts, the face
reveals us most because it most
distinguishes one person from
another, emphasizing difference,
proclaiming we are separate
and cannot be duplicated as
is demonstrated in, let's say.
a singular relationship between
the curve-line of a stolid jaw
and the steep slope that marks a bony nose
or in the way a lowered brow protrudes
or glaring eyes retreat into their shade
revealing anger or regret. Who knows?
How much of what we see is us ourselves?

But maybe my assumption about
difference is wrong—maybe
what represents us most is what
we have in common, what we share. If so,

some other aspect of the body like
the belly, elbow, knee-cap, or the foot,
might better serve as a synecdoche.

Yes, faces are too dangerous,
too easily contorted or contrived,
no matter what commiseration they
might intimate, for us to dwell upon.
Who knows what motives lie beneath
the glory of a smile, although we ache
down in our bones to trust its radiance.

So my Talmudic guess is that the Lord
won't show His face to Moses when
he passed by, blocking his sight
with His outreaching hand.
He wanted Moses to trust his own
abiding bafflement.

So only the inscrutable backside
is visible for awestruck Moses to
remember and to contemplate.
No doubt our human backsides signify
us as essentially we are—alike,
almost indeed identical in how
we are designed to suffer and to die
with two adjacent spheres—
a sassy symbol of infinity—
that can be seen when naked we depart.
fade out and disappear beyond the rocks,
united in the laughing dark.

UNCOVERING THE DARK

O ghostly rabbi,
help me to prepare the way
to drowsiness,
to merciful forgetfulness,
the earned reward
for effort in the cause
of holding on, of cherishing
what soon must disappear
not ever to return.

The inner dark, so like the outer
just before the early stars appear,
before the Sabbath starts,
before the peace that can encompass
consciousness arrives,
but only for an interval—only
until harsh moonlight
makes the hemlock shadows
shudder in the underbrush.

My mind, unable to accept
its own evasions and defeats
still hears that ghostly rabbi
chanting underneath his breath.
He chants a prayer that creature sorrows
of despairing humankind—

the hungry at the field's fenced edge,
the solitary in their speechless gloom—
be eased so wakefulness
becomes endurable.

O rabbi, hunched in breathless prayer,
teach me to make the darkened sky's
encroaching dark my own
before the loosed horse paws
its apprehension in the pasture
by an agitated stream,
that I might celebrate
the gift of drowsiness as if
to let go were a choice, as if
dark sleep is briefer than oblivion.

GRIEVING FOR ANNIE

When we behold a wide turf-covered expanse, we
should remember that its smoothness, on which so
much of its beauty depends, is mainly due to the
inequalities having been slowly leveled by worms.
—CHARLES DARWIN

Prolific Darwin is remembered for
his ailments and his generosity
toward loyal friends, consideration for
his wife's life-long religious faith,
devotion to his many children,
Annie in particular, who died
of fever at the age of ten.
　　Darwin's commitment to the truth
of how Nature designed itself, based on
observation and analysis.
Evidence, despite the consolation
offered by a Christian after-life
that needed to be given up, provides
a model for the tolerant of stomach
and the unequivocal of heart.
　　Darwin's great theory of selection and
Descent how creatures struggle to compete
since their supplies of food are limited—
is the most powerful idea ever
conceived by humankind because
of its explanatory scope and depth:
we all remain at heart what once we've been.
Species will flourish in their time,

become extinct when circumstances change,
and vanish never to return again—
a truth excruciating to accept.
   Darwin thought evolution had produced
"forms beautiful and wonderful."
The "war of Nature" was a process
he described as having "grandeur"
since increased complexity had led
in time to human consciousness,
society, and moral sentiments
like sympathy, benevolence, and trust.
   But Darwin's attitude about how
Nature operated to select the fit
kept darkening until, disburdening
himself of pent-up anguish, Darwin
wrote to Joseph Hooker, his good friend,
condemning Nature's works as "clumsy,
wasteful, blundering, and horrible;"
no consolation for inevitable
conflict can be found except perhaps
through human care and tenderness,
the pleasure that we sometimes take
in bringing pleasure to someone we love
as little Annie surely did for him.
He wrote an elegy extolling her,
"It was delightful to behold her face,"
recording her last quaint and gracious words
as "I quite thank you" when he held
her head and offered her a final drink.

And yet it's dubious that evolution
can account for such unselfishness
or tell him where to look for consolation
in a world where loss, unmerited
and indiscriminate, seems absolute
beyond repair or recompense.
Surviving Annie's stupefying death
Darwin continued to be burdened by
the marble weight of mournfulness,
and yet he went on working since his work
allowed for self-forgetfulness
and granted him the patience to endure.

Twenty outreaching years after her death
Darwin composed a book in praise of worms,
comparing them to gardeners who
"prepare the ground for seedlings of all kinds,"
depicting worms as cultivators—first
among the farmers of the earth.

Did Darwin find some consolation in
the laboring of lowly worms who plowed
the soil for ages immemorial
in knowledge of renewal through decay?
Could such relief suffice for him
and ease the ache of his undying grief?

CROSSING THE BRIDGE

For Stanley Bates

When old age shall this generation waste,
Thou shalt remain in midst of other woe
Than ours, a friend to man, to whom thou sayest:
Beauty is Truth , Truth Beauty,
That is all ye know on earth, and all ye need
to know.
  —from "Ode on a Grecian Urn," JOHN KEATS

And now it is my generation
that has gone to waste.
I have outlasted my best friends;
no one is left but me
and this elusive, talking urn.
So I will play along with this
engaging fantasy as if
the late philosopher Stan Bates
and his exploratory mind were here
to tease me with the concept of
statically engraved eternity
and help me to distract myself
from the engulfing sense of emptiness
by thinking about thinking while
assuming thought is able to
protect us from the thoughts we think:
discoursing with a meditative urn,
conversing with you when you are not here.

I will interrogate the urn
by asking what it means by its
notorious and enigmatic claim
that Truth and Beauty are identical,
and I'll conjecture that the far side
of the urn, the side I cannot see,
shows a tableau of a familiar scene
in early spring of a carousing stream
still edged with a fine filigree of ice
and highlighted with puffs of mist
like miniature ghosts. Across the stream
a tree has fallen like a walkway
for a spirit, should he need a passage
to the undepicted shrubbery
beyond the sleek stones on the other bank.
The spirit is, of course, invisible,
as you are now, but I can hear
his wafted flute notes as he passes by
in lilting harmony with the swirled stream's
incantatory whispering—
as Keats could hear soft sweetness in
the silence of those "unheard melodies"
and I can hear you praising the audacity
of Keats's baffling paradox.
I'm guessing that you would agree that this
impressionistic woodland scene
is beautiful and I'd be pleased to have
the urn give it artistic permanence,
but since all permanence is an
illusion, the urn's vain assertion
in undoubting certainty

cannot be true, yet knowing that
it is not true—nothing is true
that does not change and disappear—
surely is true, despite our wish that we
might be less permanently sorrowful,
and sorrow no more than a shadow
on fresh snow, the murmuring of wind
amid the drying meadow grass.
But I cannot delude myself or long
be unaware of the surrounding emptiness,
pretending that you're here and we
are entertained by speculating what
the urn might understand about
our need for solace in its offering
of friendship to its onlookers.
Stan Bates, philosopher, is gone—he is
not here on earth to quip he is not here.
Consummate connoisseur of classical
conundrums, maestro of mimetic mirth,
steadfast, devoted, generous—it's true,
as well, he was a realist of woe
for whom grief was the bond for all of us.
And I think that is beautiful.
There is a slender, sloping bridge
of wooden planks and wooden rails that I
have crossed a thousand times on my way home
and paused to watch the white-tailed deer
come out to drink, arpeggios
of water sliding silver from their lips,
and I can recollect those seasons when
determined beavers made a dam

and built a hutch, a perfect dome
Euclid himself might have designed,
and once at dusk, but only once,
I saw a pygmy owl swoop down
on soundless, outstretched wings
to snatch a vole beneath the snow,
his golden eyes like harvest moons
whose radiance delineates the dark.
I'd need a million, eulogizing urns
to keep such earthly memories alive,
even for just a fleeting interval—
as if, dear Stan, they could be kept for you.

SLANT APRIL RAIN

slaps on my window
which looks out beyond a valley
of old crowded evergreens
to mountain peaks
that seem to shudder
in the surging wind.

Complete unto itself
upon a marble tabletop
below the misted window glass
glistens an azure vase
with daffodils that lean
toward recollected sun.
A yellow spider, almost
imperceptible, reposes
at a petal's lilting edge,
preparing to move on according to
an immemorial intent.

How pleasurable it is
to speak its name—
Yellow Sac Spider—
and to cite the fact it feeds
on a variety of flies
whose chemistry determines
the surviving spider's
versatile display of greenish hues.

I pause to marvel at
this minuscule spectacle—
a sight remote from anything
pertaining to my personal
rewards or grievances,
my satisfactions or regrets.

And so I watch the spider
on the petal of a daffodil,
and I too am suspended in
the shadow of its pausing there,
Surely the spider has
somewhere to go beyond
these daffodils composed
within their azure bowl,
and, thanks to him,

I offer up this little parable,
while stationary here,
of momentary solace for all those
who seek a purposed way to go
as slant rain rages blindly
in the mountaintops.

MY POLITICAL DEBUT

The thump I made with that big gavel
on the Speaker's resonating desk
reverberates down to my bones
when I recall that day—
I'm guessing I was twelve years old—
my father, then a New York senator,
arranged for me to aid the Chair
begin a session of the congress
at the capital in Albany.

A day's drive from our home
in our Bronx neighborhood,
the district represented by my dad,
the highway leaves already had begun
to curl and turn a muddy brown,
and at a stoplight where the road diverged,
a beggar with his patient dog
held a hand-written sign that read:
YARD WORK EXCHANGED FOR FOOD.

Dad got the names confused of ballplayers,
our favorites, and yet I didn't think
to ask him if he was okay
or if he wanted to turn back.
We drove in silence as the dusk came on..

I didn't understand all that
preliminary talk or what
exactly "anti-vivisection" meant,

but when the Speaker leaned toward me,
explaining that the bill to be discussed
would save innocent animals
from scientists' experiments on them
that caused them awful pain,
I knew I should say something since
I'd raised and cared for many pets,
including guinea pigs.
Though I felt awkward sitting there
where everyone could watch,
to my astonishment
I asked the Speaker if I could
address the audience.
And wow! flushed with a flow of words
I hardly knew that I possessed,
I told that gloomy room of senators
that laws for being kind to animals
were their responsibility;
I told them animals can suffer
just as much as people do;
chimps hold each other if one is in pain;
I told them that the earth
belongs to every creature living here.

        The senators applauded me
and one said that some day
I would be president. And yet
my speech defending animals
concluded my career in politics.
I don't think that the bill got far enough
to even come up for a vote.

On the long journey home,
my father's thoughts seemed far away;
I was afraid to ask if something
might be troubling him,
if something I had blurted out
in front of all those senators
might have embarrassed him.
Shortly before arriving home
we bumped into another car—
a minor fender-bender—so he had
no chance to offer a reply,
and we decided that we'd keep
the accident just to ourselves.

And now, a lifetime later
that's included a World War,
Korea, and Vietnam,
no president was able to prevent,
I can imagine the destruction
yet to come. At home in our own land,
with hatred in accusing voices
that believe others are guilty
of transgressions which reside
in their own hearts, how can
fresh kindness be revived in us
and quicken in our iron wilderness?

Not counting my persuasiveness
with senatorial authority,
the little power I possessed
I've spent by helping my good wife

in parenting our children who
needed protective kindness too,
as do we all—no other rescue
from a barren destiny in sight—
as did my father who abided with us
only four more dwindling years,
not time enough to say farewell.

EPITHALAMIUM

For Dan and Pat July 11, 2015

Early in March, Erik my son, and I,
and Dan and Pat, caretakers
of the wilderness, set forth
to view Montana's Freezeout Lake
where thousands of Snow Geese
stop off to rest and feed before
continuing their journey north.
    Astonished, with long arms outstretched
like a Blue Heron's coasting wings,
Dan watched sleek geese descend
in dense coordinated swoops, then circle
and return to the illuminated lake;
together we observed the Tundra Swans
glide silently as if they knew
they were admired by us
and need not hasten to depart
as long as their suffusing glow
ignited our own flowing thoughts.
    Before our transfixed eyes
the streaking swans seemed motionless
as if composed in a tableau
arranged that instant as
an unrepeatable design,
like the design that brought us here,
our mutual delight in spectacle.

We marveled how their pattern
constantly revived itself
until the moment came for them
to fade away on their illuminated wings,
departing from our sight
that migratory season in
its swirling Freezout interval.
    Collective awe had bonded us anew
so that in time and telling
being there and being gone
will not be seen as separate
when once again we share accounts
of how the incandescent swans
propelled black-footed bodies up
from the reverberating lake.
    Remembered springtime merges into now,
and now we gather here to celebrate—
full summer humming in our bones—
the promises of loyalty
encircling what elusive time
makes precious in the urgency
of knowing that we must at last
relinquish everything we love
to the indifferent air.
    Briefly among us congregated
on the breeding earth, we come, we go,
along with plants, with trees, with birds,
with butterflies, with animals—
Pat's shiny- eyed-endangered Pikas
huddled on the Glacier mountaintop,

guardians at the border where
protecting cold is needed
for their pulsing bodies to survive.
    And now vermillion light bears witness
to our witnessing, this wedding feast—
the vows that carry us beyond ourselves
in this suspended interval
like the ascent of disappearing swans,
even beyond what we can see.
As you, dear friends, are unified
by consecrated words, so are we all;
with our winged words we're able to
make manifest the rapturous idea
of fellowship, fulfilling right here
in this cherished place of keeping watch,
of water mirroring the mountains
and the sky, what we, alive,
have always wished—that our own wilderness
of fertile wishes may endure and thrive.

SPACE

While contemplating the full moon
and how it seemed to give
delicate substance to surrounding space,
sending concentric circles streaming out,
I looked down at the shadows
of the intermingling firs and pines
delineated on the snow
so vividly that they could be
etched there as if intended to
remain unaltered and unchanged.

I felt the moon's ancestral spell
which stirred my mind with musings
about curving forms, the circle,
things complete unto themselves,
resolved and permanent.

But then, as if arising from the shade,
a phantasm, my white-haired stepfather
appeared as when he moved in
with our family—my mother,
younger sister, and my sixteen-years-old
high school self, just one year after
my own father's death by heart attack.

My stepfather had grown up poor
with shoes that always were a size too small;
he graduated junior high
then had to get a full-time job

as janitor in a men's clothing store,
but after forty years of
selling trousers on the road
in undistinguishable towns,
he saved enough to purchase stock,
and he became a partner
in the company, providing him
with means to woo my mother
out of dependent widowhood.

      The two possessions that he brought with him
were a huge leather chair and ottoman
on which to rest mis-shaped feet
and his prize wide-band radio
to listen to the news each night
with commentary and advice
he offered to his unseen
and approving audience.

      One night, after ex-astronaut John Glenn,
who had become a candidate
for public office and was now
expounding his own principles
of justice, economic growth,
and necessary work,
my stepfather exclaimed
"What I admire about this man
is that he is so down to earth."
Was he aware, I wondered then,
of his comic profundity?

Aroused to inadvertent eloquence,
he sermonized to his imagined
wide-band audience
on the ennobling trials of poverty.

But there were only us three to attend—
my mother and my sister and myself—
just old enough to see my mother's
uncompleted mourning in her eyes,
and see at bedtime my young sister's
pale, abandoned look
of having been betrayed
by her first father's early death.

For sure, that was quite down to earth enough,
I thought while watching the full circle
of the moon become
the silver sliver of an arc
and disappear behind a cloud—
a shape without a name, with nothing
it can be remembered by,
even forgetting that one does forget
except to be aware that nothing's left,
nothing but the night air,
the stillness of the still night air.

I WELL REMEMBER

When I told my wary wife-to-be
the story about how it got decided
where I'd go to college. That's when,
though she might disagree, she first
warmed to my amorous attempts.
　　My parents took a cottage by a lake
while I and my small sister went to camp
that summer when my father had
his final stroke. He would slip in and out
of consciousness, attended by
a sympathetic nurse, so my
exhausted mother could have time
by herself and leave the house to shop
around the nearby town. But she had trouble
following directions, just as she often
mixed up people's names, and so
she got back late that afternoon
barely in time to hear her husband blurt
his final words above the sobbing nurse:
"I want Bobby to go to college
in New Hampshire, in the mountains
among gentlemen of promise," though
I doubt that "gentlemen" is a word
my father likely would have used.
　　He was an immigrant from Germany
and had to take a job to earn enough
tuition money for the law school
he attended after work at night
in turbulent New York,

according to my grandmother's account.
And so Dartmouth was where I went,
and though I did appreciate the little town
of Lebanon, and did enjoy
the clear night sky whose constellations
I could name, and took long solitary walks
along the riverbank, I missed the city's
swagger and its swirl, the opera,
the company of girls, and told my mother
that I'd like to transfer to Columbia.
But she was adamant: "Dartmouth
is where your father wanted you to go,
and Dartmouth is the school from where
he would want you to graduate." So I
remained at Dartmouth just as fate decreed.

    Some five years later, married, and now
living in New York, my mother,
worry in her eyes, treated me to lunch
at an expensive restaurant. "Bobby,"
she said, "there's a confession
that I've got to make, a burden
I have carried way too long. It wasn't right
for me to tell you not to transfer
to Columbia; your father would
have wanted the decision to be yours."
"That's in the past, Mom," 1 replied,
"it can't be altered or revised."

    More years, more aching years pass by,
and once again my urgent mother
takes me out for lunch. "Bobby," she says,

"it still upsets me when I think that I
prevented you from switching colleges
and moving to New York; who knows
how that affected whom you chose
to marry, your decision to return to school,
what kind of a parent you've become."
Again I hear myself pontificate:
"We must accept the past for what it was;
it's like one's having read it in a book."
Another interval unwinds.
To my annoyance and astonishment,
my mother, with the same look in her eyes,
returns to her regrets. "For God's sake, Mom,
that's ancient history," I interrupt,
"just let it be!" "But there's more that I
haven't yet confessed to you,"
my trembling mother manages to say,
"I never should have left the house
that afternoon, and I'm not sure exactly
what your father's last words were.
"Williams" is what he might have said."

MEADOWLARK

A view to set against oblivion,
Gold-blooming balsamroot illuminates
The mountainside and circumscribes the one
Noteworthy, preening meadowlark who waits

For my approval then begins again
As if his melody within my mind
Is also needed by grouped angels when
They are assembled listening to find

Heavenly satisfaction in a sight
So season-bound and so ephemeral
In the contingency of golden light
Made manifest in a bird's lilting call

Resounding through the vibrant April air
Complete and ultimate, just being there.

PICASSO AND ME

I have a friend who has a friend who knows
the curator at the Modern Museum;
the friend contacts my own friend informing him
the curator knows of a Picasso portrait
of himself about which there is doubt
concerning authenticity.
　　The story that's associated with
this self-reflective work involves
my friend's friend as potential customer
insisting that the painting should be
verified—Picasso must confirm
the portrait of himself as his own work.
　　A viewing is arranged, and after
careful scrutiny, Picasso claims,
or so the story goes, "Let me
assure you, sir, that I can paint
a fake Picasso just as well as anyone."
"So what the hell am I to make of that?"
my friend's trustworthy friend, replied,
and he declined to purchase it.
And yet, surprisingly he urges
my impressionable friend to buy
the painting as a good investment
even as a forgery, although, with luck,
it might be genuine. He hands my friend
a glossy photograph of the oil-thick
self-portrait which reveals the subject's eyes
as strikingly uneven and askew;

the mouth is represented by
a thick black line emphatically grim.
My friend, judiciously suspicious, asks
why might Picasso consider it to be a fake
even if he himself had painted it?
Was it an imitation of a style he thought
he had already mastered and outgrown,
or had he then depicted sorrow that
he did not feel the day he painted it?
And yet, my friend, from true experience,
Was able to identify with it—perhaps
it reenacted some betrayal by
someone he once trusted long ago.

     The curator had claimed, "there is no way
that one can guess Picasso's motive in
suggesting that his painting was a fake;
maybe he's been unfaithful to someone
he cared about, and now he feels remorse."
My friend suspects the curator
in consort within his friend perhaps
have plotted and have pre-arranged to get
a big commission on the painting,
whether fake or not, if it is sold, and yet
my friend dislikes himself for thinking this.
The lack of focus of the eyes, he thinks,
might well imply evasion of some kind;
maybe the curator's interpretation
was a confession of some hidden guilt?
The tight lines of the silent mouth
could readily convey something unlawful

pressing outward to reveal itself
My friend assures me that he is ashamed
by wayward thoughts like these that thrust
themselves in his impressionable mind.
It was not his intent that his response
in studying the painting should turn
cynical, and he prefers to think
Picasso did not mean that his painting
literally should be regarded as a fake,
but, rather, that it could expose anyone's
temptation to deceive himself.
    And yet those eyes, that black line of the mouth,
could mean a thousand things my friend,
or even I, might possibly project
into Picasso's comprehending mind—
his fears, suspicions, his hostilities.
    For sure, the painting had its own
unfathomably rich expressiveness,
despite the tale my friend's friend told,
resisting what one tried to make of it.
    So once again my intervening friend
peers in the eyes that looked at him
from deep inside the painting's frame, as I
look in his eyes when we converse,
as if another painting might be found,
acknowledged by Picasso as his own,
perhaps about himself, perhaps of anyone,
and I might want to purchase it from him.

ODE TO A LOVESICK MOOSE

Experts at first thought the relationship between the lovesick moose (Bullwinkle) and a Hereford cow (Jessica) was only a flirtation, but now the muzzling has gone on for nearly two months. Baffled animal behaviorists say it may be true love-at least on the moose's part. "He just has these mixed-up feelings, something between compassion and companionship," says Charles Wiley, Vermont's moose expert. . . Tony Bubenik, a retired moose researcher, said that he simply thinks the lovesick moose is a little bit immature.

The Burlington Free Press, December 26, 1986

Sing heav'nly moose, you baffler of behaviorists
of love, abiding love, beyond
    flirtation and the tease
of nuzzling Jessica amid the Hereford herd
among the sullen cedar trees
muffled with snow, beside an ice-edged stream
in star-crossed Shrewsbury, misty
    at ominous, red dawn.
Still unrequited in Vermont, you are prepared
to wait until all the snows are gone
at this appointed place, unlikely landscape
of romance, your muddy state
    between companionship
and passion, no!, is not mixed-up or immature.
Rather I see your spirit grip
its fate in this harsh world, implausibly
incarnate in your patient bulk
    so seemingly astray.

O, expert disbelievers, look at Bullwinkle,
See how he guards her daily hay
and rests his muzzle on her back, then gazes
   at the darkened sky, his love
transcending what the genes
of other species-bonded moose ever could know
even among the freshest greens
of the eternal fields of flowing spring.
Divine mutation, holy moose,
inspire new love in me, beyond my horny kind,
for the dazed cow of Earth
now grazing sunlit in my mind.

BULLWINKLE REVISITED

Back in Vermont misty decades ago
a moose the newspapers named "Bullwinkle"
arrived to hang out at a farm where he
fell hopelessly in love with "Jessica,"
a cow who was the gleaming apple of
his amorous, distracted eye.
      Resting his cumbersome, racked head
upon her back, Bullwinkle surpassed
in sentiment what his ungainly species
normally was fashioned to achieve.
Inspired by this account, I penned
"Ode to a Lovesick Moose," a poem
extolling forlorn love, which I
declaimed in elevated cadences
to a large audience that summer at
a festival of avid listeners
with their own cultivated taste for words.
      "Sing heav'nly moose," my opening
invocatory line, offered mock honor
to Urania, the muse John Milton summoned
in his epic of our primal parents' fall
into mortality caused merely by
their eating of forbidden fruit—
a punishment too grave to fit the crime.
      Light-hearted blasphemer in my
ripe younger years, I had complacent faith
that Milton's somber ghost
would be amused by my tart pun.
As soon as my most lofty phrase

had flown forth lilting from my lips
to conjure up the love-sick moose,
my pal and fellow- poet, Marvin Bell,
rose from his seat with hands cupped at his mouth,
let loose a resonating "BOO!"
as everyone joined in with joyful hoots
ascending to the shaking rafters of
the quaking auditorium.
  Who does not know that what a punster
wishes from an audience is groans—
infernal groans that can make manifest
the power to liberate our booziness
from guilty self-denial and restraint?
Never before that rousing day
had I felt so completely understood;
never had I been celebrated by a crowd
that recognized how a rebellious pun
can thumb its nose at sanctimonious
high-mindedness and glum solemnity
and still retain its cheerfulness.
  Packed full with double implications
with their cutting edges able to
retaliate against all would-be wooers
who disdain frivolity, my pungent words
depicted latent longings in my soul
as horniness incarnate in
confusion of a raunchy moose.
  Musing on how our unrequited loves
ennoble even as they humble us
with gross contortions of desire, I'm able
to renew my striving strophes now

in favor of meandering moose music
with its sweetly numbered lays
as in old choirs of ancient harmonies.
Accordingly aroused, I can affirm
the ringing pandemonium of BOOs,
believing such bravado does provide
fair compensation for those "heav'nly" hymns
that seek help from divinity as if
to rescue Nature from itself, assured
the hallelujahs we can improvise,
bamboozled and bemused, may well suffice
in seeking to amuse ourselves and rise above,
with choral wails and howls and bellowings,
in giving praise to all aspiring love.

BOBCAT AT HOLLAND LAKE LODGE

John was the longtime manager
of Holland Lodge
by pristine Holland Lake,
surrounded by the vast Swan Mountain Range
out to the east, and, to the west,
the mighty Mission Mountain Range.
    If you look out across the lake,
you'll see an incandescent waterfall,
or if you row to the south shore.
it's likely you will see
gnawed branches heaped
above the waterline
to form the arched roof
of a beaver hutch.
    You might spy white-tailed deer
descend past glinting pines
to drink at the lake's stony rim,
then pause to scrutinize
uncertain stirring in the underbrush.
    High in a swaying tamarack,
an eagle settles in her nest
with folded wings.
You could be standing here
a quarter century ago,
the year my wife and I arrived,
and see what you see now:
unfurling purple clouds,
the ghostly sliver of a crescent moon,

a family of sleek Merganser ducks
dipping in ripples
of their buoyant element,
a painted turtle basking
on a partly sunken log.
    You might imagine this tableau
had been designed by John
for every visitor's delight—
to be here without questioning,
just to observe, though it is tempting
to believe John's rapt description
of this hushed, encircled place as if
it were the Peaceable Kingdom
that Isaiah prophesied.
    One languid summer day
when I was reading by the lake,
John unexpectedly appeared
cradling a baby bobcat at his chest.
John made a blanket bed for him
inside the cabin where he lived
behind the public lodge;
and also built a cage outside
from which the bobcat could
peer out into the spangled woods
and sniff the currents of the wind.
    Though he resembled a domestic cat,
when he attained maturity,
his shoulder tendons tightened
and the muscles in his back
became more taut and sinewy.

I felt primeval power
lurking everywhere I touched.
On snowy afternoons, I'd sit
cross-legged upon the cabin floor,
and he would slink up from behind,
set his spread paws upon my back
and rub his cheek against my cheek
as if to reassure me
of our creature-bond.
       John's son had cautioned me
that stalking was the way
bobcats hunt hares and rodents
they depend upon for sustenance.
A bobcat will attack a hare
with silent steps upon the snow;
one pounce is needed, nothing more.
       John had informed me that
it was his plan from the beginning
when he brought the baby bobcat home
to set him loose to find a mate
in the remaining wilderness.
       "But what if he can't make it
in the wild?" I queried John.
"What if we have smothered
his ancestral instinct to survive?"
My apprehension must have troubled John
since it took years before, at mating time,
he set the bobcat free.
       In March the Lodge was emptied of its quests,
and John could travel anywhere he wished

although he chose to keep
his destination to himself.
　　A couple that my wife and I
befriended way back in our city days
had come for a reunion at our house.
"We haven't watched the sun
reflected on a mountain peak—
not since our honeymoon,"
his wife lamented to my wife
beside the consolation of a fire
the snowfall night that they arrived.
　　Next day I drove them the
few rutted miles to Holland Lake
to contemplate the spectral radiance
of the half-frozen waterfall,
when at the forest's birch-grove borderline,
　　I spied our bobcat crouching on a rock.
My friends could see me looking, so
they saw the bobcat too
as he charged toward us
at ferocious speed. Not breaking stride,
yet catching the effulgent light,
the bobcat leapt into my outstretched arms
as a reverberating scream
surged from my friends in unison
who clung together by
the ice-encrusted lake as if
this were their second honeymoon.
　　"That's how wild animals respond to me!"
I oratorically proclaimed

to comfort my astounded friends
that legendary day
as if Isaiah's prophecy
had finally been realized.
John never did return
to Holland Lodge;
he was succeeded by his son
who had the bobcat's cage removed,
yet laughed approvingly to hear my tale
about a forest animal
who had remembered who I was,
inspiring me to utter words
that might well serve
to sound the trumpet of my epitaph—
my celebration of a peaceful
kingdom's glistening.

ABUNDANCE

On the east shore
of Flathead lake
in northwest Montana,
weather conditions
are exactly right
for growing cherries,
and for a thirty mile stretch
sloped orchards in neat rows
of carefully pruned trees
display their luminescent blossoms in the
softening May breeze.

Abundance is the overflowing word
betokening what dazzled eyes behold
that resonates as in the sound of clover bees,
or like the thrumming wings
of hummingbirds—
as if summer could be
suspended in mid flight.

Grateful for such bounty
I improvise a goddess
bathing in a stream,
imbibing cherries as
thick crimson juice slips down
and stains the corners of her lips.

Abundance is my chosen theme,
even beyond spring blossoming—
my father placing slippers on a snowman's
head for ears
to hear his footsteps in the night;
my mother costuming our bulldog
as a ghost for Halloween;
my sister painting butterflies
across her bedroom wall
as if they landed in a lily pond.

Each image glows
within the orchard of my mind
here in Montana where
my wife and I have chosen well
to make our home
here in Montana even though
December's streaking snow
blasts native ravens
huddled on a fallen cedar fence
dreaming no doubt of ripened corm
in an open field.
And I, to conjure up
ephemeral contentedness,
must cherish blooming cherry trees
still blossoming abundantly
within the orchard of my mind.

SWAN RIVER IN OCTOBER

Shimmering crimson clouds
are now reflected on the river as
my son and I coast downstream
toward no destination
in particular. We paddle and we drift,
feeling the current in our bones,
repeating its inevitable flow.
    Ahead we see a beaver lodge
fringed with fresh branches harvested
for winter nourishment to feed
a family of six or more. A beaver
slaps the water with its thick, flat tail
which makes a cracking sound
that echoes like a rifle shot.
    And high above, three Sandhill cranes
in silhouette, with wing-spans
almost eight feet long, prepare
for immanent migration south,
forming a triangle which they maintain
until they have diminished out of sight.
A rainbow trout with its pink stripe
breaks through the surface calm to snatch a bug,
creating ripples that dissolve
expanding into circles so symmetrical
one might imagine a designer
improvised in forms that no competitor
would presume to emulate.
    My son avoids a tree stump
lurking just beneath the mirror

of configured clouds, and I can see
a vein jump in his sun-burned neck
as he swerves our wood-carved canoe
back on its course to somewhere
still to be decided as late light
begins to settle in the reeds
and in the berry-studded shrubbery.
A doe arrives at river's edge
and adds her hoof prints to the tell-tale mud;
she bows her head to drink,
then suddenly lifts up as water
tumbles from her lips; her ears twitch as
she stares in our direction though,
assuringly, I whisper we
have no desire to cause her harm—
all creatures here are safe for now—
but, unpersuaded, off she goes
into the rustling underbrush.
    And now I wonder what my son
might say to me, or I to him,
beside our tended fire tonight
within a ring of gathered stones;
does something all-fulfilling
and definitive require expression
in our human words, or can
our drifting on Swan River with
reflected cloud formations twice
glimpsed in their darkened colors I
cannot describe, sustain us
and inscrutably suffice.

ELEVATED THOUGHTS FOR PAMELA

My mother was afraid of heights,
and also is my wife and so I ask:
with such a wary lineage
what mischief in her DNA
impelled our daughter to become
a rock climber, an "off-width" specialist
who squeezes into a crevice where
she vanishes into its shade.
  But now l see her dangling
from the windy heights between
the stillness of her being there
and the abiding quietude
of red streaks and striations
in the persevering stone.
    Down on firm planet earth
my wife and I share apprehensions
that are easy to explain
as dread of helplessness;
and yet without the ecstasy
in disciplined suspension of her breath,
her almost weightless floating there,
perhaps the vast, unfathomable
uncertainty of parenthood
possesses in its dark abysmal depths
a mad exhilaration of its own.
    And there, supported by a cam,
a steel contravene fastened in
a cleavage in the stone,

she pauses in the noon-hour sun;
a wisp of moon emerges from
a rushing cloud; in silhouette
a swooping hawk dissolves into a haze
that leads to the horizon's pale,
hallucinated edge in a serenity
incomprehensible beyond
the transformations of all accident,
beyond the vigil of our fears.

ELEPHANT IDENTITY

Female elephants, seeing their babies
tumbling and playing and sleeping,
are suffused with a sense of well being.
—CARL SUFFFINA: *Beyond Words*

Since nature-bending wishes are not
Likely to come true, I have no fear
Some random misplaced consequence
Might cause me to lose sight of who I am,
and so I dare to wish to be reborn
Enlarged in a recycled life—
An elephant mother, thriving
In a protected habitat, for whom
Caretaking is its own reward
And has no need for motivating thoughts
Of obligation or of sacrifice,
Watching the tumbling and the chasing and
The twirling ears is quite enough.
The males, off by themselves, bellow and stomp,
according to upstart testosterone
That makes them all belligerent,
As I was in my youth, and driven by
The pungent perfume of desire.
Surely, resourceful evolution might
Have easily erected a device
More dignified in keeping us
Content and moderate as if
Friendliness was the hoped-for goal
That evolution set out to
Accomplish from its sexless start.

But if my wish miscarries due
To some obscure ambivalence deep in
My dreaming mind, and I'm brought back
As male, too hopelessly conditioned
By the life I have already lived,
Then let me be a father seahorse
Carrying to incubation all
Those sticky eggs passed on to him
By his enlightened paramour, his body
Animated with ongoing usefulness
    Or maybe I should optimistically
Return for one more try at being male,
Even as a bull elephant,
Although an elephant in "mutsh"
Has little choice of how to act
And little range of what to feel—
Benevolence or else hostility.
But if I can't escape becoming
Human once again, assuming my
Particularly named identity,
    I'll seize the freedom of some interval
When roused testosterone abates
So I can celebrate the fantasies
Revealing who I am at heart
That carry me beyond my given self,
Beyond my fated creaturehood,
Before I'm destined to resume
My intermittent role conceiving kids.
Not everyone can be a pachyderm.

EPISTLE OF MOTHER BONOBO
TO HER DAUGHTER

I can imagine you are reading this
by the reflecting pool where first we two
were summoned by the voices in the wind
that left us trembling, wary and confused.
We females were wisely created with
the brave ability to organize
so our coordinated strength can thwart
aroused, aggressive males from acting out
their amorous demands against our wills.
  This strategy has worked for us
as long as anybody can recall,
but rumor has it now that right across
the mighty river separating us
are chimpanzees, as they are called, that look
so much like us but freely copulate without awareness
of their fatherhood.
  My daughter, I don't know what we would do
if males like these should take control right here
because they're physically superior and can
coerce us merely with their potency.
Maybe they'll turn their strength against each other
and then somehow we'll become entangled
even in their fiercest rivalries.
  That silent fear is what disturbs my sleep.
So here's what I suggest—ally yourself,
not only with your daughter, but also
with your son, chasing his brother

through the underbrush, a stick in hand.
and howling unconfined delight,
or crouching where the waterfall cascades
upon the rocks, casting a rainbow up
above the swirling spume, transfixed,
wide-eyed, and harmless even for
a brief, prophetic interval as he bears witness to the
glowing spectacle.

INCREDIBLE BEAR ENCOUNTER

I took an unfamiliar path
into the tangled wilderness.
the elevation higher, and the air
just thin enough to make
my breathing somewhat difficult
and cause my intermittent view
of the vast Mission mountain range,
the valley plummeting below,
to seem a hazy blue in swirling light.
I stumbled on a fallen branch
and think I may have hit my head.
as from behind a vaulting pine
a giant grizzly bear appeared
who reared upright in front of me,
his sickle claws stretched out,
saliva dripping from his teeth.
I know you can't outrun a bear,
and though I am an atheist,
I figured that my only chance was prayer.
"Lord!" I exclaimed, my face
raised heavenward,
"If You will intervene to spare my life,
protect me from this mighty bear,
I promise that I'll read the bible with
an open mind right to its scary end;
I'll make a generous donation to
The Wilderness Society;
I'll be more sensitive in choosing
whom to tell offensive jokes."

"Not too convincing," I acknowledged
to myself, yet that's the best
I could come up with on the spot.
The bear took one step closer,
stared at me, then lifted up his eyes
to scan the sky, and in a language
I, incredibly, could comprehend,
he said "I thank you. Lord for this fine meal,
this blessing that Your bounty is
about to graciously bestow on me."
      That very instant all the leaves,
the aspens and the cottonwoods,
stopped quaking and went absolutely still;
the nearby stream ceased tumbling in its flow;
a pillaged woodpecker desisted
in his echoed hammering;
clouds thickened, and the sky closed in.
      I realized I could not emulate
the bear's sincerity
and that I had to improvise
a more persuasive strategy.
But I know nothing of the purposes
a deity might have in mind
in making all-consuming hunger
the first, universal motive
of all living things, or why chance is
a factor in the way events turn out.
      But knowing that I do not know is all I could be certain of.
If someone up there might be listening,
it's sure that he or maybe she wants to remain inscrutable,
and what can possibly

be more inscrutable, I thought,
than my escaping from this bear
or that the bear should suddenly
turn peaceable? And so, content
with my intrepid reasoning,
I felt secure that I could rest my case.
    When I awoke, the aspen leaves
again were quaking in the wind;
the stream was foaming over purple stones;
the woodpecker resumed his hammering,
but on the tree above my head,
illuminated in a lunar beam,
I saw a silver tuft of fur
where the great bear had rubbed his back,
perhaps to ease a sudden itch, and then
had disappeared into the underbrush.
Incredible as it may seem,
I felt a pang of apprehension in the bear's behalf:
for how in hell
can he survive, with his gigantic appetite,
unless he has enough to eat?

QUACKERY

When I was just a carefree boy
President Roosevelt did not allow
A boat of Jewish refugees to land
And settle safely in America,
 I bought a duck I named Enrico for
His resonantly operatic voice.
I kept him in our heated barn,
And every morning I would walk
With him only a step behind
Along a wooded pathway to a pond
Where he would coast and drift,
Content, it seemed to be a duck,
Although, by virtue of adoption, an
Ethnically authentic Jewish duck.
At dusk I'd stroll back to the pond
And call his name; he'd come at once
And strut in step with me back
To the barn to sleep and no doubt dream
The simple wishes good ducks dream.
 One day, at summer's end,
I went to summon him,
But he did not return despite
My pleading calls, and I assumed
He might have gone off with a lady duck—
That's natural enough—though maybe
A weasel snatched his slender neck,
And that, I fear, is nature too.
Three quarters of a brutal century

Has slithered by with multitudes
Who vanished unconsoled, unmourned,
My powers of caretaking are gone,
Though not my need to care,
To go on caring to go on.

  And now my smooth imaginary duck,
Whom I've named Quackery
Accompanies my evening walks
Through the encroaching shrubbery
Down to a pond with sunfish gulping
By the cluttered lily pads.
I call to him by his newest name to ask
If there is anything he needs,
But he is happiest just drifting
On the pond, then circling back
With his responsive echoings
To where he has already been
And still at heart desires to go.

  Now in his wake quivering ripples are
Ignited by the risen moon,
And now a hesitating wind
Among the branches of a row
Of willow trees on the far bank
Composes what I hear as weeping sounds,
Though maybe they are sounds of some
Mysterious repose—serenity
Of gradual forgetting, letting go.
Soothing, and liltingly melodious.

TRICK OR TREAT

It's Halloween and he's alone
when at his door a woman
in a mask, dressed all in black—
black velvet cape and shiny gown—
knocks at his door. He has been reading
how black holes, just like the one
in our own galaxy, suck in
neighboring stars that get too close
to its event horizon—so it's called;
everything disappears, forever
lost, forever unretrievable.
She steps across the threshold
of his entryway and scrutinizes him
a blue vein pulses in her forehead as
she opens up her gown as wide
as her stretched arms can reach
and stands there naked as the moon
light seems to radiate from her—
from everywhere that he
allows himself to look. She whispers,
"Trick or Treat" in melancholy tones,
but it's not clear to him if "Trick""
is meant to have the connotations
as in "turning tricks" and therefore
means about the same as "treat,"
implying pleasure wholly sexual
or if "trick" means the opposite of
"treat," suggesting painful punishment

for some infraction of Kant's
categorical imperative
requiring abstinence or self-restraint,
but ignorant of consequence,
unsure of how she might respond
he can't decide . . . Immobile he
stands stiffly staring—for how long
he can't tell—until she vanishes
into the trembling midnight air.
  He's lost track of the years gone by
though here he is again on Halloween,
still faithful to the moon, still true,
waiting to see if she will come again
and if he'll get a second chance.
Perhaps this time he'll know instinctively
what choice to make—or maybe
she will indicate a preference
for how she wishes he'll respond
to mitigate uncertainty
like the enigma of what's to be made
of an owl's gliding silhouette
crossing the window glass from where
he now waits patiently to watch.

SNOW SCENE WITH RAVEN

Wet clinging snow accumulates
On aspen branches, birches, tamaracks,
On cedar fences that delineate
The silent fields, the frozen stalks

and barren brambles that express
the tangle of what shapes remain.
Whiteness, unifying whiteness,
Extends, diffuses, and contains.

The icy dazzle of its glittterings.
An interrupting raven clamors past,
Its gold eye vivid in a blur of wings;
This pang of darkness cannot last.

I'm here where all temptations come to go,
Enraptured in oblivion of snow.

DEFIANCE

What can defiance salvage in the end
to show that we indeed were here
though not for long with easy time to spend,
except in song, except in lilting song?
The limping last Tyrannosaurus Rex
watches the dust-infected sun descend
as if blurred light intended to perplex
beyond what flesh can comprehend,
incapable of laughter or despair
when driven by blind appetite whose laws
lack urgency to space out breathful air,
to make it rises and make it pause.
And so I'll beam out into cosmic space
a Bach chorale that at a wishful guess
will find a listener or else out-face
the unresponding face of nothingness.

MIST

So many truths to choose among,
To pluck out of the air, and yet

One doesn't get to speak one's last words last,
to summon up a final quip

That makes acceptance seem acceptable,
Allows one to repose in restlessness.

An owl sits on my window ledge.
Beyond the ridge coyotes close on their kill.

Torn trees are creaking in the wind,
Swaying as if they're eager to depart.

What would my long-gone father say
To share my isolated gloom?

Would my abiding mother's words
Rise up to testify in my behalf?

And which me represents me best
Of all those clamoring to be recalled?

The brash, rambunctious youth
Or this slight self grown quiet and morose?

My numb legs barely hold me up;
My walker wheezes at its servitude.

My vision hazes over and my ears
Hear voices from forgotten rooms.

Would I feel better if I could blame god
For how my body has decayed?

Is frailty a punishment
Heroically to be endured

In rebel opposition to
Indifferent Nature's laws?

Ephemeral, pain is ephemeral,
And pleasure too: the grinning pumpkin head

With candles fluttering for eyes
And evening mist descending with

Remaining leaves that curl upon
The foaming currents of a stream

Where otters improvised their slides
Down shiny mud-packed banks. And yet

I tell myself I should not make
This story autobiographical

Or try to recollect things as they were
In strict, delineating light.

It's certain I've not spent my life
As if my history were mine alone;

Impersonal awareness silently
Accompanied my journeying

Although my wordless self trudged through deep snow
One swirling January night to reach

My friend's log house because I knew
That he would need my company

After his brother tumbled into the lake
Watching the moon descend

To meet its own reflection on the ice.
Or maybe the reverse is true,

Maybe he was the one who braved a storm,
And I the one in need who, having climbed

Up through deracinated ice,
Had made it back alive that misty night,

Whichever truth is actually true.
It now lies smothered in the past.

So all that now remains lives only in
Retelling of a story told,

Of mergings and relinquishments
That spread gray shadows over lips

And over eyes like mist descending
On the windows of a distant house—

The dark house of a stranger or
Perhaps the dark house of a friend.

TAMARACKS REFLECTED IN A LAKE

The only evergreens not always green,
with pale November coming on,
green tamaracks will more and more,
though almost imperceptibly, let go
their needles to the forest floor.

October now displays its hues,
as if the autumn season can
encompass coming forth and going hence
as one and give a lilting ease to thought.
and give to thought a longer span.

Green needles brighten in their mellowing:
yellow turns gold, gold shades to denser bronze,
repeated in the rippling lake,
so slowly over dwindling days
that I can comprehend transfigured trees
as if they've been designed
to go their modulating ways
to barrenness their vanishing contained
within my momentary gaze.

The beauty of these evergreens
in their prolific letting go
repeated in the trembling of the lake
which seems to cherish them,
preparing for the silence that I know
is soon to come—the silence
of stark branches underneath
the silence of accumulating snow.

In stillness I can let myself
serenely listen as green silence
diminishes toward dull oblivion
devoid of yellow, gold, or bronze,
reflected only as a memory,
until all going finally is gone.

GOLDEN TAMARACKS

About to drop their brittle needles,
golden tamaracks have reached
the peak of their effulgent glow,
and so my son and I decide to drive
up to the hidden lookout site
where we'll enjoy a panoramic view
of the illuminated mountainside.
We take a twisting forest road
to the outcropping precipice from where
we can enjoy the valley trees aflame
and scan the snowcapped Swan Range stretching out
and disappearing into purple haze.
Whether it was the higher altitude,
the jarring logger road, or else
the vista's dizzying magnificence,
its plunging contours and its shifting
modulated hues of gold, my chest
contracted and began to palpitate.
I sat down on a stump and waited as
my son ran to our truck to get
some nitroglycerin and place a tablet
tightly underneath my tongue.
The vista trembled, and the golden light
splattered upon my hands and arms;
I watched my son receding as
he waved farewell, and maybe he
was beckoning me home and then
I thought I heard him call to me,

but I could not make out his words—
were they just the rumble of the wind?
    The agitated clouds reflected light
back to the blazing mountainside,
increasing its intensity, its shimmer
and its radiance—as if I'd crossed
a border to another realm too bright
to fix my burning eyes upon.
    When I returned, I found myself
still seated on the stump, my legs
splayed out, my arms supporting me,
my son now just a breath away.
    "I've never seen the tamaracks
sustain their radiance so long,"
my son said as we drove back home
over the deep-grooved forest road
with its attending raven scavengers,
November shadows emanating
from the tangled underbrush.

SNOW GHOSTS

Montanans call them Snow
Ghosts—globs of snow
accumulated on the trees,
especially the evergreens,
and clinging there
immoveable in frigid air.
　　You've got to live back in the woods
without another house in sight to hear
the silence underneath
the quietude that radiates
from muffled snow,
from smothered leaves.
　　I cannot find the word
that best describes
the eeriness of this effect
of silence deepening—
silence of primal nothingness
preceding the emergence
of the melancholy humming
of unfathomable space,
the so-called music of the spores.
　　This forest stillness is enticing
and yet frightening—not fearful
like marauding wolves,
but like a lone, disoriented wanderer
seeking to find his way back home
for whom silence is
no longer so impersonal.

He is my speechless double
who cannot resist the pull
of silence toward finality,
the heat death of the universe,
the equilibrium of entropy
after the inevitable passage
to oblivion, devoid
of memory that we were here,
without awareness
even of our suffering.
    I call to him, but there is no reply.
He lifts his arms toward me
as if to touch my face,
and stumbles silently
beneath the misted window glass
in drifted snow.

BEAR GRASS INTERVAL

At roughly ten year intervals
this globe of minuscule white flowers
clustered on a dense green stalk
appears profusely in the vernal woods
of mountain-range Montana,
so the entranced observer stares
at what appears to be
a galaxy of stars that has now drifted down
and settled softly on the earth.
　　Ask anybody who has witnessed
this phantasmagorical display,
and they will swear
that they have never seen
a spectacle so tranquil
and serenely beautiful.
　　Yet I imagine beauty
here on earth does not
originate in the beholder's eye,
but dwells out there inherent
 in the humming universe
as one of Plato's fundamental forms
beyond the realm of time and space
that still can harmonize discordant thought
and woo the tides of the recumbent air.
　　You ask how this far-out belief
affects my life; am I
less self-absorbed and less defined
by personal diminishing
to primal and concluding nothingness?

Perhaps if everyone would pause
to gaze upon the Bear Grass flowers
glowing on the mountainside,
and view them as if willfully designed,
a combination of sweet symmetries
and startling randomness,
then they would feel less separate,
less lonely, less irrelevant, content
to play the quiet role of witnesses.
    But now, right now, the galaxy
of Bear Grass flowers is not visible
 and will not reappear
for an uncertain interval,
assuming earthly time
still measures disappearances,
the emptiness lost love and friendship leave
forever achingly behind.
    I do not know if I'll endure
another interval—a wandering
beholder of the momentary woods—
until Bear Grass returns to grace my sight
and holds there, astounded
and suspended in delight.

WATER MEMORIES, WATER DREAMS

When I was twenty-one
and hiking up a mountainside
to reach a waterfall
a girl walked with me.
We were holding hands although
I did not try to kiss her, thinking
that she might reject my overture.
Her mind unknown to me,
we sat together on a fallen tree,
watching the waterfall spin out its foam
above the darker current underneath,
forever changing, always the same,
constant in its inconstancy.

Years floated by, and resting on a ledge
above a swimming hole gouged out
by a cascading stream,
I saw a father with his son
appear and leap together
 in the churning pool. At once
the father was sucked down
although he managed to thrust up
his writhing son above his head
so I was able to grab hold of him
and host him safely back on land.
The father disappeared so rapidly
I couldn't find him when
I dove in after him. His body
was recovered the next day

bolt upright in a whirling vortex
with his arms outstretched as if
he still were beckoning for help.

Another outpouring of years,
and there I am canoeing in a cove
observing feeding ducks dip down
then shake themselves and preen,
their shimmering green heads
resplendent in mid- summer sun.
I strip down to my underwear,
slither into the lake and swim across,
not caring how I will get back.

One umber fall I walk out on our dock
to watch the geese in wedged formation
test their wings in preparation for
their migratory journey south.
I look down at still water and I see
my own reflection in the lake;
a sweat drop from my forehead falls
and ripples outward from my face
as if intending to reveal
a purposeful design.

To this day I still dream
in water images, and I suspect I may
have once been rescued from the sea
when I was maybe two years old—
the summer that my parents
rented a log cabin by the shore

according to my mother's memory.
I asked her if she let me play
in the wet sand collecting shells
among the skittering of sandpipers,
but all she let herself recall
was that my father was not well
and that she had to care for him.

Again last night I had a swimming dream.
Too far from land, I felt
the pulsing of the universal tide
and felt the ocean rise as when
first separated from the firmament.

I woke abruptly from the dream
with curled waves unfurling at my back
and ventured forth into the hazy air,
into the rain that falls
upon the rich and on the poor,
upon the young and on the old,
on women as on men,
on all the virtuous, all the corrupt,
on humans and on animals,
upon the joyous and the sorrowful,
skeptics, believers, and the searchers
who are certain only of uncertainty:
all are alike at heart, including me—
we all are interchangeable, and so
without complaint, without regret.
without some distant place to go.
I have no wish my life were otherwise.

GRANDPA'S LAST SEDER

"We knew we'd have to leave our home,
despite our garden and our friends—
Russia was far too dangerous for Jews,"
was what my grandpa said
as I helped blow the candles out
after the Seder ended late as usual.
    Grandpa conducted the ceremony
without a single word omitted or
a single rousing song unsung,
as my unspoken blasphemy
from boyish restlessness replied,
"We could have walked across the Sinai
and then half way back."
But grandpa's oratory soared
above my restlessness,
beyond his speech impediment.
    A red-cheeked, robust man,
he must have been deprived
of adequate nutrition as a child,
since in the new country,
his name for Brooklyn Heights,
where the whole family set down new roots,
no longer did he have natural teeth
which were replaced by an entire set
of almost perfectly symmetrical
but often clacking dentures,
so at regulated intervals,
no doubt to give his mouth relief,
he'd put them in a glass of tea—

the magic source, he claimed,
of his unfailing confidence that all
adversities can be endured.

  Grandma amused herself by telling us
how grandpa's grin would greet her
from their bedside table
to begin the duties of the day.
and that sometimes she'd see
his smiling dentures in the sky
amid familiar constellations
of the very stars that Abraham
believed predicted his posterity.

  At the last Seder that he led,
untiring so it seemed to me,
now half asleep, he improvised,
right at the end, a sermon of his own
from what he had inherited:
he pointed out that nowhere
in the Haggadah—the guide
for every Seder's rituals—
was Moses recognized by name,
although his presence was felt everywhere,
contending with the pharaoh's wrath,
then leading the afflicted Hebrews
out from demeaning servitude
to face new trials in the wilderness.
I pictured Moses leaning on his staff,
hoping someday he'd reach the holy land;
and it occurred to me that his bronze face
resembled grandpa's face,
and his stutter, caused by putting

a hot coal to his lips when just a child,
thinking that it was good to eat,
reminded me of grandpa's handicap.

As Moses' life was rounding to an end,
and still not having reached the holy land,
the Lord, as Moses set it down
in Deuteronomy, confronted him:
"I lay before you life and death,"
blessing and curse,
choose life that you may live,
you and your children
and your grandchildren."
Having recited these hard words by heart,
Grandpa paused momentarily
and looked at all of us together
in one brooding glance, and then,
as if he swooned into a trance,
he added, "Yes, in spite of death's
unrelenting permanence.
in spite of universal suffering,
in spite of hatred inescapable
and everywhere." I gasped,
for there before my eyes stood Moses
as Grandpa's tightened smile returned,
a thin, straight line across his lips.

As he had unmistakably foreseen,
one night the uniformed police
smashed down their door, ransacked their house,
and stole their heirloom candelabra
made of antique silver and engraved
with detailed workmanship.

They slunk off with the gilt-framed portrait
of my grandmother when she
had reached a womanly sixteen.
Grandpa sold everything he could
and hired a coach on the next night
to take them to the railway station
of a nearby town. On the next day
they made it to Odessa,
then the next to Warsaw,
then to Amsterdam, and finally
across the thundering Atlantic
on an old commercial steamship
to Montreal where a year passed before
they could obtain the faded visas
that enabled them, my mother,
her twin sisters, and a brother
too young to recall their frantic trip
at last until, as grandpa promised,
all of them could celebrate
a Seder in Jerusalem.
But they, as destiny decreed, remained
in Brooklyn Heights near Prospect Park,
and there they opened up a restaurant
where Grandma was the chef supreme
and Grandpa greeted customers by name.
Grandma would tell them what to eat,
"Tonight the pot roast!" she'd proclaim,
as Grandpa, toasting everybody's future
with a resonating "sei gesund,"
would praise the soup—"like wine,
the soup is sweet as honey wine
exactly as it is in paradise."

That final mystifying Seder night,
as if for the first time, Grandpa expounded
how the barren wilderness,
and the Egyptian soldiers in pursuit,
compelled our ancestors, in mortal haste,
to eat only unleavened bread,
so that we now dip matzo in red wine
in order to commemorate
their hardships and their suffering.
    And then Grandpa looked off in silence
to imagine some far country where
I could not follow him, perhaps
the self-same country Moses would
not be permitted to set foot upon...
There stood Moses with his staff
that had brought water from a rock,
right there in Grandma's dining room;
it was as if his words became
my Grandpa's words, though I myself,
not knowing if I had the fire
to make them mine, and thus
appropriately humbled, possessed
astonishment to apprehend
what had transpired before my eyes.
And when, a stranger to myself,
closed in unfathomable gloom,
which like nature's own seasons comes and goes,
I find unspeakably within my heart.
the wish to kill, the wish to die,
    I look up at the patient stars
where I can see grandfather's dentures

gleaming in the spectral night
like a remembered constellation
suddenly emerged from a dense cloud,
about to disappear again
as greeting interchanges with goodbye.
And I can hear inherent laughter
or high lamentation in the wind
as if Grandpa had spoken
a farewell for me, for everyone,
words I can cherish as my own
wherever I might chance to lay my head,
those terrifying, those momentous words:
CHOOSE LIFE.

COKE BOTTLE AT DAWN

We were four high school buddies and
for thirteen years without a break,
starting as sophomores, we gathered
after Labor Day for a reunion
at the Preston family estate
on Martha's Vineyard's southern shore.
with its eroding, shrub-strewn cliffs,
where Roger's regal mother kept her watch.
We'd spend a glowing week cavorting
in the amber sun and body-surfing
among sandpipers skittering along
the fractured, conch-bespangled beach.
At night we re-enacted our
heroics on the football field,
catches, and tackles, and elusive runs
as pompom, white-thighed co-eds
cheer us fabulously on.
There was a log-hewn cabin in the woods,
hidden from the majestical main house,
where we hung out, Roger and Woody,
Gilly and I, provisioned with a propane stove,
an old GE refrigerator, and
a Zenith radio for current music which
inspired us to romp and dance,
and brought distracting news about a military buildup in
some unknown country overseas.
Rumors warned that a draft of all Americans
without deferments, such as ours, was imminent.

A shore-eared owl inhabited the splattered attic over us.
She seemed to tolerate our presence there
as if she knew we would not stay beyond the time allotted us.
    We took turns shopping for supplies—
Roger and Woody, Gilly, and I—
for dinners that were easy to prepare:
hot dogs, cold cuts, canned beans. Bond bread, and spam
fulfilled our need for banqueting
as we lit candles in the dusk.
And all we asked the spirits of the ocean
to provide was somersaulting waves
to float our bodies through the buoyant foam.
    One day I failed to bring back our
required supply of coke. Woody loved coke.
"It's my elixir," he proclaimed,
"It clears my mind and gives me stamina."
Gilly complained the water in the cabin
tasted stale with rust, it made him sad,
though I suspect it was the limp mouse dangling from
the owl's hooked beak that saddened him.
That night Roger and I drove into town
where Roger knew a distribution plant
displayed a ten foot Coca-Cola bottle
at its entryway. Made of green plastic,
it appeared ignited by the moon.
Filled to the tapered top with sand
that held it steady in its place,
its bottom was a plywood board
we easily removed so we
could tilt the bottle on its side,

empty the sand, and haul it off
as if it were a genie's residence—
a giant genie whose wish-granting power we
could employ and harness as our own.
We loaded it into our jeep
and whisked it to our cabin in the woods.
We propped the bottle right outside
the window above Woody's bed so, when he woke,
he would be sure to see it radiating there
in the vermillion light of streaming dawn.

    Woody's wild outcry of astonishment—
as if the cosmic fount of plenitude
had been revealed to him—
that shook the cabin to its earthly roots,
still echoes in my memory
and sends a shudder of delight
back to the marrow of my
bones, although each humbled
and decrepit one of us,
Roger and Woody, Gilly and I,
are scattered by an unexpected wind
into a country where reunion banquets fade
and are almost dissolved in mist.

    Roger's family's ancestral house,
its stretch of periwinkle beach,
have shadowy decades ago been parceled
into lots where once a pod of whales
inscrutably marooned themselves
and had to be removed by grunting tugs.
God knows what devastation is in store

for humankind with demonic Korea
stealthily ensconced across the sea
the way distance is calculated now.
    The distribution plant is gone.
and I cannot locate whoever might
have saved the great coke bottle
as a souvenir. But if I close my eyes
against the bare, September sun,
I still can picture our attending owl
peer at us in her cabin loft,
and I'm still able to recall
the thunderous vibrations in the air
as Woody's outcry in that legendary dawn
unwound beyond the looming cliffs,
beyond the continent, beyond the sea,
past Jupiter and past Uranus,
out to the edge of our Milky Way,
or, possibly, for all I know, by now
it is departing from Andromeda.

EMBELLISHMENT

Although old age is new to me,
I feel I'm getting better
in the art of letting go,
relinquishing enjoyment in
the wind's embrace, the sight
of redpolls at the birdfeeder.
Nothing now happening seems actual
except when it is, improvised
according to some urgent need.
I am familiar with familiarity
and I do not regret
my story might be happier.
The limits of the possible
have surely been confirmed.

Yet here I am right now,
sitting beside my garden pond,
leaning my head back on a willow tree
I planted years ago,
watching the steady sun ignite
the yellow flowers on the lily pads.
A shiny frog pops up to breathe,
her golden eyes survey the scene
including 20,000 eggs
that clump together on a lily stalk,
her contribution to posterity,

I call to her in my
best booming imitation of
a bullfrog paramour,
transformed into a prince of this
prolific kingdom of fertility.
And in this moment of my frog
identity, I banish from my mind
the life I've lived, the human question,
whether anything I know
about myself or what I've done
is worth preserving or
best honored in forgetfulness.

So I interrogate the wind
to ask should I attempt
to cherish in deep memory
this ordinary day
in which two dragonflies appear
suspended right above a sculpture
of a mermaid covering her breasts.
Again I bellow out in my
best bullfrog operatic baritone
to shake whatever empathy
lies in the confines of her heart,
but in reply there's only
the green silence of the lily pads
With her wide smile, the lady bullfrog,
as indifferent fate decrees,
is not impressed and won't consider
I might be an eligible suitor of
most royal bullfrog lineage.

Why not? What's wrong, I ask myself,
with such revisionist embellishment
upon the everlasting theme
of wishing to be thus transfigured
and redemptively renewed
as evening mellows in my garden plot
and casts the shadow of the willow tree
out over the entire lily pond?

HUMMING IN THE AIR,
FLUTE MUSIC ON LAND

I'm drifting slowly in my wooden boat,
observing turtles sunning on a log,
seeing how close I can approach
before they plunk, like a plucked violin,
into the lake and disappear.

I shiver with the pleasure
of just being here, measuring
my afternoon in turtle intervals
of vanishing—when suddenly
my disappearing turtle trance
is interrupted by the thrumming
of a streaking heron's wings
and my heart's pulse becomes
the down strokes of extended wings.

I sense a soft vibration in the air
as if a choir were humming
in a cloud, an intimation
at the core of quietude.

My boat glides closer to the shore
and I can hear a tanager's faint trill
passing so quickly that I am not sure
it really fluttered there
in shifting intermittent shade.

Murmuring ripples on the lake waft in
and then the swoosh of wind
among a canopy of pines.
descends and settles in the underbrush.

And I am wondering
what my rapt presence adds
as I pause here between
those painted turtles on their log
and their swift vanishing
into their silent element.
between the heron's flashing
and its blur diminishing beyond
the blue horizon's borderline.

Perhaps our evanescent universe,
red-shifted to infinity,
requires a listener,
a wide-eyed observer, someone
to behold his own beholding here,
right here beneath our minor sun.

There on the pebbled shore,
a flute raised to her lips,
a slender barefoot lady stands
about to play, and playing,
and already having played,
her silver notes float toward me over
glintings on the surface of the lake.

Mellifluous, they flow as if
intending to make music mean
much more than meaning
ever previously meant—
repeatably repeatable,
like circles in their circularity,
serene, and permanent.

PASTRAMI IN PARADISE

*Zabars may well be the best Jewish
delicatessen in New York.*

Now that I have late leisure time to spend,
I'm able freely to meander
among cloudy speculations whether
in some frequented neighborhood
in paradise one still can order
a pastrami sandwich on rye bread.
And drowsily I wonder if my mother,
having settled in for the long haul,
still makes heroic matzah balls
to celebrate the holidays.
      I can remember her dyslexia,
how she'd confuse the names
of the male members in our family
and call me Carl, my father's name,
or call her grandson (on my sister's side)
Bobby, yet every one of us was certain
to reply when summoned by her.
      I recollect the day when Jamie
told her that the Peace Corps offered him
a full-year's fellowship to study
tribal rituals in Africa, and, anxious
to the marrow of her Jewish bones,
she phoned me to inquire
what foods the natives eat in Africa:
"Isn't starvation a big problem there?"

"But where in Africa," I questioned her,
"has Jamie been assigned?"
"It's a huge continent." She paused,
and then she answered, "Zabars, I think
Zabars is where they're sending him." "That's good,"
I cheerfully replied, "there's nothing then
for you to fear; he'll come back home
at least a few pounds heavier."
 A half a century has failed to dim
this vivid memory, and now
I'm wondering if the distracted Lord
enjoys a saucy anecdote like this
with its intrigue of interchanging names.
And when my mother's turn comes round
to stand before the holy throne,
will she repeat the questions
that disturbed her mortal days?
 Will she, in her dyslexic innocence,
address the Lord as Joseph, her
own father's name—Joseph
who never let his tea grow cold—
to ask if loss, her husband's early death,
somehow had been required
in the elusive scheme of things
for her love to attain full vigilance?
 On her refrigerator door, as if
engraved in stone, my mother pinned these words:
IN TIMES OF HAPPINESS, EAT HEARTILY;
WHEN SORROW COMES, ALSO EAT HEARTILY.
I see her in her comfortable shoes

and the white apron that my grandma wore;
she hands the Lord a sandwich for His lunch—
pastrami with a pickle on rye bread.
"Ess! ess!" she urges Him, "I know You still
have cares that need revisiting."

SANDHILL CRANES DANCING

for Patty

At dawn the Sandhill cranes, their heads
splashed vivid red, initiate
their mating dance, circling each other
on long, narrow legs tanning their huge, gray wings
in slow, dreamlike deliberation.
    They throw sticks from their pointed beaks
into the air to flaunt their mating skills.
Their whooping echoes out across
the same dew-sparkled field
where they've returned each spring
for twenty years since we, my wife and I,
initially began to keep our watch.
    A forest ranger we'd not met before
stops by our house to ask if we have seen
the grizzly bear tracks in the mud
beside our border stream. He tells us that
the constellation Ursa Major will
appear tonight effulgent
right above us in the northern sky
and that he likes to stay awake at night,
with just his telescope for company,
to calculate how long it takes
red-shifted light to reach the earth.
"My favorite is melancholy Saturn,"
he declares and its attendant moons,
each one with its own orbit, hue, and size.

My hope is that I'll find a hidden moon
that no one has observed before;
it would preserve my name."
   He says that stars right now are being born
and burning out, collapsing on themselves,
that due to universal entropy
in maybe fifty-million years
all matter will thin out and dissipate,
so that no memory and no
intelligence—none would survive.
   And even I, who own no telescope,
can comprehend terminal emptiness;
it's no less thinkable than is
next May without our being here to watch
the cranes perform their dance as if
their tossing sticks into the dawn
and catching them might signify
that everything returns again
to re-enact past happiness.
   Yet in our bones we know that soon
our bearing witness must conclude,
just as the green field must turn brown,
which it, alas, has been designed to do.
So let us pause again in misty light
to watch those red crests blur and disappear
above the waving trees. and listen hard
as medleyed crane calls float away
and fade into a murmur in the air.

PERFECT RAINBOW

Driving me home from yet
another visit to the eye doctor,
my wife took the old farmland route,
and there across a field of corn,
stretching from east to west,
a rainbow's arc appeared;
uninterrupted and connecting
earthbound base to earthbound base,
its glowing colors merging yet distinct,
perfectly symmetrical, it shimmered there
ascending heavenward, descending back.
I wondered how I might regard
this biblical display, the admonition
from Leviticus requiring us to leave
unharvested a measure of the crop
at the designated far edge
for the unfortunate and destitute.

Before my tearing eyes, the field of corn,
swayed by a sudden surge of wind
became transformed into a roiling sea,
and I looked out, as Noah had,
to see a perfect rainbow beckoning,
assuring him dry land would soon appear,
that life would long continue for his wife,
his sons, the coupled animals.

But then the rainbow disappeared
behind accumulating clouds,
and my imagining myself as Noah
dissipated into evening gloom.
though I imagined ragged figures
crouching at the border of the field.
I wondered whether Noah wondered
what vicissitudes awaited him
 and his attending family
when he descended from the ark,
what fate awaited all those animals,
who no longer would be in his care.

When we arrived back home again,
my wife helped me into our house where I
could rest beside the animated fire
of red and yellow flickering.
My dog lay his moist nose upon my feet;
my cat leaped to my lap, curled up,
and purred as if she were in paradise.
Lightning lit up our windows with a flash;
thunder resounded in the rafter beams,
and it began to pour in silver waves
as rampant wind besieged the trees
and pounded hail stones in the flower beds
although the house itself felt water-tight.

My wife rushed over to the kitchen door
and opened it against invading wind
as, two by two, the animals came in

and shook themselves: the white-tailed deer,
foxes and wolves, red squirrels, bobcats,
beavers, otters, skunks, and antelope,
and quail and grouse, turkeys and short-eared owls,
and, yes, of course, brown bears came too,
and thick-necked grizzlies with their mighty claws.
"It must have been the rainbow," my wife said.

All One Breath was typeset in Minion, an old-style serif typeface designed by Robert Slimbach of Adobe Systems and was released in 1990 by Linotype. This typeface encapsulates the aesthetic appeal of the Renaissance and the exceptional readability of typefaces of the day. For this reason, Minion has proved to be a popular font for on-screen use. The inspiration for Slimbach's design came from late Renaissance period classic typefaces in the old serif style. The Renaissance period was noted for its elegant and attractive typefaces that were also highly readable. The name Minion is derived from the traditional classification and naming of typeface sizes, minion being a size in between brevier and nonpareil. It approximates to a modern 7 point lettering size. The overall appearance of the Minion design is very much related to the appearance of mass-produced publications of late Renaissance but there is an added touch of classic typography design not possible with older, inaccurate print machinery. This new take on those old styles has produced a crisper outline. The Minion typeface family has been expertly crafted to retain great readability by producing a print clarity that even the best of the Renaissance typographers could not manage.

DESIGN BY DEDE CUMMINGS
BRATTLEBORO, VERMONT

CPSIA information can be obtained
at www.ICGtesting.com
Printed in the USA
LVHW041927050219
606517LV00002B/3/P